Unsent Texts To a Local Loser and other Musings

Amanda Skaja

BookLeaf
Publishing

India | USA | UK

Presentation by *BookLeaf Publishing*

Web: www.bookleafpub.com

E-mail: info@bookleafpub.com

ISBN: 9789358318661

First edition 2023

DEDICATION

This is dedicated to everyone who learned the hard way what "unconditional love" meant.

ACKNOWLEDGEMENT

Thank you D for loving me just enough to understand what love really is. I never wrote poetry until I needed to figure out how to describe how I felt after you.

Soon... be patient.

Someday, soon,
I think...
I'll get to say
"I told you so"
but...
I promise
I'll refrain...
probably.
The last three years
will make sense
shortly.
knowing is a burden when you are impatient...

That's how "Unconditional" works...

The more books I read the more okay it becomes to love someone who can't say it back. Because that's what we're meant to do, love our selves and love each other…. Without conditions…. So if you haven't been told lately (or even if someone tells you daily) you are enough and I love you.

(hashtag sh*tty poetry)

Loving you is easy
but not very convenient
when I crave the touch
And something intimate
Someone to be proud of
And who will also share my wins
Or even the hard times
And when we cry
Loving you is by far the easiest
And hardest at once

The Restless Nights...

What is on my mind
I'm restless and have been up for almost 24
hours
My stomach in knots for the last few days
Anxiety I can't explain
But I can't stop smiling either
When I sleep I dream of the same person
Some in great detail
Some just flashes of his face
Maybe I'm losing my mind
Cuz I hear him say he misses me
And I feel him grab my hand
A kiss on my right cheek
Or a body wrapped around mine
That should spook me
Normally that'd spook me
But it feels safe

Hey Mr. Potato

5

Hugs from potato head
Good vibes only
I've been very stressed
But changes come hopefully
Soon we'll see
Get over this hump
Trust the
Processssssss
Live laugh love.

How I know!

When our first date was, in fact, a date and I was not upset by it. When you read my tarot and your interpretation was more fluid than mine (I have gotten better though), when you said you wanted to "make love" to me (or do you say that to all the girls?). When I explained how my depression shows up and you told me you thought I was great as you kissed me on the side of my head (it was such a warm moment). When we followed the sunset and I said "the only problem with bangs is they have this awkward stage where they are consistently in your eyes no matter what.." and you gently pushed them aside (just for them to fall back immediately after, I'm sure). When we sat above the town and I took your hat and we talked about the Timbers night. When you hugged me in my room, and I said "you're the perfect height" and I'm just now thinking your response was just… "you're perfect…" When I told you my weird restaurant bathroom anxiety (why did I tell you that? I've never told anyone that!) and again when you offered to find the women's room for me. When we had already spent an entire day together and we were hugging in your bedroom and I said

"when you get bored by me just let me know,
and I will go home without feeling offended…"
and you responded with along the lines of "I
could do this forever" (it probably was not that
but it was to that effect). On New Year Day 2021
when you told me you missed me and maybe
you were crazy too. (Because I would apologize
for being crazy).
I'll always like you but I'm getting better at
ignoring it. (Am I really though?)
I think you'll always like me and you're finding
it harder to ignore.
Are you confused why you like me still? I'm
not, but I'm the heart where you're the brain.
You can't use logic to navigate love. It won't
ever make mental sense. Let go of trying to
make it.

First Kisses

I stepped outside to take my dog out once more before bedtime. And the atmosphere felt calm like before that first real kiss. When you can tell this person will stick with you a long time. The anticipation growing because you've thought about kissing them many times before. The warmth. The secrets you will pass between you in this very moment though a word will not be said. The softness you can't wait to feel to fall into. I stepped outside and was pulled back to your room. Cherry Chapstick. Thank you…

Hey Drummer Boy

I saw you recently
Maybe it's just my
imagination
But when you saw me
your face lit up,
boyish and pure.

Hide-aways

Running away to the forest may not solve your problems but it does give you time and space to ease your mind. Grounding and connecting back to nature. Learn to be wild, again. Trust your instincts better. Sit by a river. The flow and sound kind of hypnotizes. Summertime. I'm ready....

Who is who, maybe we're one.

Yin and Yang
The darkness cannot exist without the light
The moon cannot shine without the sun
I can exist without you
But I'm the prettiest when I remember how you
reacted upon my late arrival to our first date
The expression on your face and the glittering in
your blue eyes
The calling me some form of "pretty" or
"beautiful"
That sly and overwhelming kind of suspicious
smile I wear
Just a stamp of a memory or more
Where I remembered suddenly
What it felt like, finally, to be the most beautiful
woman in the room just because you looked at
me....
Thank you for loving me when we didn't even
realize that's what we were doing yet...

Potato Headed fool....

12

I see the men I thought I loved once
Because I used to be the girl that
fell for everyone
And they aren not cute anymore
But when I see you. Your dumb bald
head looking like a giant potato
I can't help but to smile
Because even then, you're still cute to me.

When we meet again.

Maybe someday when we meet
again. We can talk about the ways
we've hurt each other until
we run out of things to say...
Forgiving each other
then never bringing it up anymore.
We are different people, now.
Maybe someday when we meet again
we will meet as strangers, all over
with a hint of familiarity.
We won't have to regard our past
because we know that's not us anymore
Maybe eventually when we meet again
our separate worries about meeting again
will just melt away because we missed
each other too much to care.
Maybe we will meet again, and
when we do,
let's just trust that our souls
will know what to do.

Where I was, and when I forget You

The plan I had in mind was to walk slowly and calmly into love with you. It was supposed to grow over time as if neither of us knew, already. Learning to talk openly about what we needed and wanted without feeling embarrassed, or afraid it would blow up into an argument. Accusation thrown around "what? Am I not good enough"
"I'm ready to fall in love" I declared to the universe before you came along. Not knowing that I had to be more specific about "and to have him stick around longer than a few months…"
But I also knew better. Cuz when I wasn't sure if you were asleep I wanted to whisper "you're going to love me when you're ready" like I knew already you would leave. And I already knew better when I planned on asking you not to ghost me when you fell in love and freaked out about it. Two hours before you dumped me. And when I thought I was fine because I didn't cry. And when I finally cried but it was because I couldn't see your dog. "You're gonna be my dog one day" I told him by accident before you broke up with me.

And I thought I was fine because even though I
missed you I thought "well we belong together
and he'll realize soon… he said he had feelings
and he doesn't get feelings that won't just 'go
away'"
And then I wasn't fine. I saw you with another
girl. And I wasn't fine. Spiraling cuz I didn't
understand I wasn't fine. That one morning New
Year's Day when I thought I'd be okay sooner
that later and I said a normal thing to you and
you told me you missed me. I still wasn't fine.
Trying to ignore what I knew for months and the
months turned to years. And I'm doing better
and most days I'm fine. Until I get too
comfortable being fine and begin to forget.
Dreams of you.

Are we connected?

As I shut my eyes
to go to sleep
I asked:
"What are you afraid of?"
And without hesitation
A response was made
"shutting down when things get har or;
when I don't know how to deal with an emotion"
and I said
"well this is a good start, I can work with this..."
and fell asleep soon after...

Not that I was counting...

I've been called a lot of things
In reference
to my looks
but nothing beats
when you called me "pretty"
like.... five times....
on our first date

You're the best at seeing them... Fishing

Went to the river
Sat in the shade. It was quite
Nobody was out today
I sat and asked for an answer
Laid down to rest a little longer
Looking at the sky
Just really wondering
Bugs kept landing on my leg
Which made me itchy
So I sat back up
And a moment later
A fish jumped out of the river
I was giddy and outwardly excited
And a moment later I saw one swim through the
water
I tried and tried every time I'm at the river
To see a fish
And once I stopped trying so hard
I saw two
And as I began to try again it they stopped
showing themselves to me
And in not so subtle ways
I got my answer.

"Stop trying and what you want will show itself…"

Moon glows

The sun kissed the moon
"My darling it's time"
And the moon felt like the prettiest moon in the
galaxy that night.

Love Letters <3

The letter you write to them after they break
your heart to a million pieces is typically filled
with mean things they did or the annoying habits
you couldn't stand. I read the letter I wrote,
"Dear ___" it began. And as I read the thing that
was supposed to talk right from the heart every
bad thing that tore me apart, instead I read
understanding. I understood why things could
not continue at the time because I myself wasn't
even wanting to date anyone quite and I
mentioned how I was taken by surprise. I read
flirtation as I mentioned before we dated,
knowing his artistic passion and how I wanted to
show up for him prior to dating, maybe he'd
notice. My admiration for the way he kept busy
with his art form along many paths and had
something quite possibly solid, then. I read
adorations. And I read an admission, the first
time I mentioned accidentally falling in love. I
didn't mean to but I wrote it because I felt it. I
read about his laugh, his smile, and the way he
mentioned "wanting to impress me" and as I did
I saw his face, and heard him. I wished him luck
and told him hopefully we'd find each other well
again. And for something so filled with

heartache it was truly, the most beautiful thing I
ever read. And when I got to the end. "Love
always Amanda" I cried and had to wonder if as
I mentioned… "I don't think this is how our
story ends…"

Fall Equinox Shadows

23

I really used to dread
the darkening sooner
and sooner
part of the year,
but it's such a good place
 to become
more in tune with
yourself….

hey you're great...

24

I want to admire
you
across   the
      room
while   you
think
 I'm just being
a creepy little
      weirdo….

Unsent texts to a local loser

25

Unsent texts to a local loser
and notebooks filled with other musings
things I'd like to say to you
Or things I've probably said anyway
Things that made me think
"oh hey he'd like this"
or things about you I really miss....

www.ingramcontent.com/pod-product-compliance
Lightning Source LLC
LaVergne TN
LVHW021354200726
843509LV00014B/2849